TREES

Clare Hibbert

PowerKiDS
press

Published in 2016 by
The Rosen Publishing Group, Inc.
29 East 21st Street, New York, NY 10010

Cataloging-in-Publication Data

Hibbert, Clare.
Trees / by Clare Hibbert.
p. cm. — (Adventures in nature)
Includes index.
ISBN 978-1-5081-4591-2 (pbk.)
ISBN 978-1-5081-4592-9 (6-pack)
ISBN 978-1-5081-4598-1 (library binding)
1. Trees — Juvenile literature. 2. Trees — Identification —
Juvenile literature.I. Hibbert, Clare, 1970-. II. Title.
QK475.8 H53 2016
582.16—d23

Copyright © 2016 Watts/PowerKids

Series Editor: Sarah Peutrill
Series Designer: Matt Lilly
Picture Researcher: Kathy Lockley
Illustrations: Andy Elkerton

Picture Credits: Alamy/David Gowans 28T; Dreamstime.com/
Alan_smithee 8TR, Andrej Tominac 19, Anest 15, AnurajRV
5, 21, Anthony Baggett 9TR, Anton Foltin 23, Artesiawells
12L, Baloncici 21, Berndlang 29CTL, Bruce Macquen 7TC,
Colombo4956 23, cpphotoimages 4B, Dannyphoto80 29, Dariusz
Kopestynski 21TR, Dave Mcleavy 9TL, David Watmought 19,
Exposureonature 13RC, Fermate 15, Gan Hui 19, Geddy 29,
Gloria P Meyerle 9CR,Hel080808 26, Hinicaise 28BL, Hittrann
19, Ichip 19, Janprid 20B, Jeffdait 23, Jesse Kraft 8, JinfengZhang
27(e), Johnsroad7 23, Joshkho 18T, Katey Jane Andrews 21,
Laboko contentts page, 17, Lian Deng 7CR, Maisna 11BR, Marco
Valdifiori 7BL, Marjancermelj 9, Masic75 23BR , Melinda Fawver
17, Melonstone 27(c), Miroslav Hlavko 19BR, Natalia Kurylo
19, Naturablichter 25TC, Neutrino89 29TR, Onefivenine 29C,
Revetina01 17BL, Rocky Reston 9, Shijianying 19, StuartPearcey
27BR, Svetlana Ileva 15, Swissmargrit 9, Sytrus 16L, Tundephoto
contents page, 21, Twilightartpictures 19, Vasilyok 18B,
Volodymyr Byrdya 25, Wirepec 24B, Xalanx 7TR; iStockphoto.
com/ Rickochet: 25; Shutterstock.com/1000words 11CR,
aimy27feb 13C akiyoko 17, Alessandro Zocc 13TL, Anatolich
27(d), Armin Staudt 5, Bildagentur Zoonar GmbH 14, Bos11
19, Bronwyn Photo 7BR, Bule Sky Studio 7TL, Crepesoles 21,
D.Kucharski K.Kukarska 27(f), Davemhuntphotography 25,
DinkaSpell 5, docstockmedia 21, DonLand 6, Elliotte Rusty
Harold 25, filmfoto 5, George P. Choma 27(b), Gertjan Hooijer
11TL, Henrik Larsson 27(a), Hjochen 15, Ina Rashke 13TR, iva
24T, Ivonne Wierink 11BC, Jan Miko 10, Jorge Salcedo 13LC,
Jukka Palm 5, Kittichai 5, LehaKoK 22, LianeM 12BR, Madlen 17,
Maks Narodenko 21, Marques 17, Martin Fowler 5, Matt Ragen
11, Mega Pixel contents page, 15BR, Mr Green 15, Nat Berth 21,
Neil Hardwick 15, Ninell 21, Noah Stryker 17, r.classen 8C, Robyn
Mackenzie 17, S, Mercer 5, Schlegelfotos Front Cover, Scisetti
Alfio 15, 17, Shelli Jenson 7BC, Tatiana Volgutova 21, Twenty20inc
11TR, unpict 20, V.J. Matthew 21, Vibrant Image Studio 4TR,
Vitaly Ilyasov 25, Volker Rauch 16B, Walid Nohra 11CL.

Manufactured in the United States of America

CPSIA Compliance Information: Batch #BW16PK: For Further Information contact
Rosen Publishing, New York, New York at 1-800-237-9932

Can you find
SIX
blue acorns hidden on the pages?

Clara is out looking at trees. Can you find her?

There are lots more puzzles in this book. You can solve them by reading the text or by looking closely at the photos. The answers are on page 30.

Contents

The great tree hunt

Trees live all around us. They grow in gardens and parks, in towns and in the countryside. Trees are a kind of plant – they are living things that can make their own food. Most plants have roots, stems, and leaves. The tree's roots hold it steady in the ground and suck up water. The tree's stems are its trunk and branches. They join the roots to the leaves.

There are three types of trees -- broad-leaved trees, conifers, and palms. They each have different kinds of leaves. Broad-leaved trees have wide leaves. Conifers have narrow leaves. Palm trees have big, stiff, spiky leaves.

Palm trees are native to tropical parts of the world.

This parkland has a mix of broad-leaved trees and conifers. The trees were planted a few hundred years ago.

Tree groups

Look at these trees. Can you tell what kind of tree each one is? Is it a broad-leaved tree, a conifer, or a palm?

coconut

oak

European larch

beech

Scots pine

Japanese maple

Norway spruce

date palm

lime

THE TREE HUNT CHALLENGE

Make a tree map

How many types are in your local park?

Broad-leaved trees

Broad-leaved trees have wide, flat leaves. Most broad-leaved trees drop their leaves in winter or when the weather turns hot and dry. Trees that lose their leaves are called deciduous trees. A few types of broad-leaved tree are evergreen. Two examples are holly and laurel. They stay green all year round. Broad-leaved trees grow fruits around their seeds.

In autumn, the leaves of deciduous trees turn from green to orange, reds and brown. Then they wither and die.

Seasons and trees

Deciduous trees look different in the different seasons. Can you figure out the season for each of these trees?

cherry

horse chestnut

American beech

hornbeam

black poplar

lime

Losing leaves

Most broad-leaved trees lose their leaves in autumn. Some drop leaves in very hot, dry weather. It is easier for trees to survive extreme cold or heat when they are dormant (in a kind of sleep). But without leaves, trees cannot make food energy (see page 16).

Many broad-leaved trees shed their leaves and then "sleep" all winter.

Conifers

Conifers have narrow leaves. Some are called needles because they are so thin and pointed. Others are small and scaly. Most conifers are evergreen. Their leaves are tough enough to cope with cold winter temperatures.

Like broad-leaved trees, conifers produce seeds inside fruits. Their fruits are usually hard, woody cones. The cones open when the seeds are ripe and scatter them into the wind. Yew is different – this conifer produces seeds inside red, berry-like fruits (see page 20).

Lumberjacks chop down trees for timber.

Conifers grow more quickly than broad-leaved trees, so they are a useful source of timber (wood). Timber from conifers is called softwood. Timber from broad-leaved trees is called hardwood.

Forests of conifers grow in cold parts of the world. This pine forest is in the US.

Conifers up close

Here are some close-ups of conifer.

Can you match each one to the right tree?

a

b

c

1

Leyland cypress

2

juniper

3

monkey puzzle

THE TREE HUNT CHALLENGE

Sniff conifers

Find some conifer needles and crush them – do they all smell the same?

Tree Shape

Poplars grow tall and thin and oaks grow big and wide. Every tree has its own typical shape because of how its branches grow. The surroundings affect the tree's shape, too. In a forest, trees grow tall and narrow to reach the light. On a cliff top, trees may grow lopsided, because of the strong winds blowing in from the sea.

This tree is growing on a windy hilltop. Over time, the strong winds have made its trunk grow sideways!

Typical shapes

Norway spruce

weeping willow

Have a look at these different tree shapes. Can you match the trees to the outlines below? Which ones are conifers?

cedar of Lebanon

Lombardy poplar

English oak

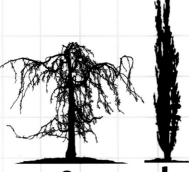

a　　**b**　　**c**　　**d**　　**e**

How people shape trees

People can change the shape of trees. Most hedges are trees that have been pruned into shape. Pollarding and coppicing are special ways of cutting trees to make new shoots grow. Pollarding is cutting off the branches. Coppicing is cutting the trunk down to the ground.

Pollarding

Coppicing

11

Bark

Tree trunks have a tough, hard outer layer of bark. Bark does three important jobs. Firstly, it stops the inside of the tree from drying out. Secondly, it protects the inside of the tree from pests. Thirdly, it stops cold or heat from harming the inside of the tree. Under the bark, tubes carry the tree's food, which is called sap.

Young trees have thin, smooth bark. As trees grow older, their bark thickens and has patterns. The patterns form because bark cannot grow or stretch. It has to split, peel or crack as the wood inside the tree grows outwards.

This spectacular bark comes from a Scots pine tree.

The cork oak's bark is harvested to use as cork.

Brilliant bark

Here are six examples of amazing tree bark but the letters of their names have been jumbled up. Can you unscramble the letters to figure out which trees the bark is from?

kelvoza mel

rapep-karb pleam

versil chirb

Euneproa hebec

wobrain cautepulsy

clue box
If you get stuck, you can find the unscrambled names here.

rainbow eucalyptus
weeping willow
zelkova elm
false elm
paper-bark maple
European beech
silver birch

THE TREE HUNT CHALLENGE

Go out bark rubbing
....
Which trees have the bumpiest bark?

How trees grow

Every tree starts from the same beginning – a seed. A seed needs soil, moisture and warmth so it can germinate (start to grow). A small root pushes downwards and a shoot pushes up to the surface. Here, the first leaves open out. The seedling grows all summer. Broad-leaved seedlings do not grow in autumn and winter because they are in a kind of sleep.

This acorn has sprouted into an oak seedling.

Winter buds

Over winter, a broad-leaved tree seedling just has a bud at the end of each shoot. Next spring, the buds open and new shoots grow. Can you match each winter twig to its outline?

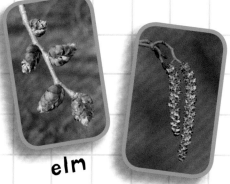
elm

alder

magnolia

beech

wild cherry

walnut

sycamore

a

b

c

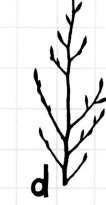
d

e

f

g

Wood

The young tree's stem slowly develops into a tree trunk with different layers of wood. The sapwood is just under the bark. It carries water and minerals from the roots. New sapwood grows each year. Old sapwood becomes the heartwood in the middle of the trunk.

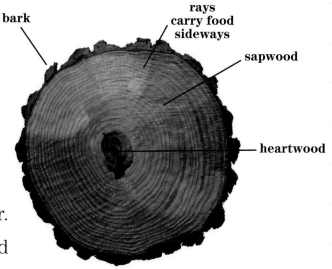

bark

rays carry food sideways

sapwood

heartwood

This cross-section shows the inside of the tree trunk.

Leaves, needles, and scales

Different trees have different leaves. Some broad-leaved trees have simple leaves – leaves in just one piece. Others have compound leaves, which are made up of smaller leaflets. Conifers have different types of leaf, too – narrow, needle-like leaves, or small, scaly leaves that overlap.

Whatever their shape, leaves are green because they contain a substance called chlorophyll. Like all plants, trees use chlorophyll to make food. The chlorophyll mixes sunlight with carbon dioxide from the air and water from the roots to make sugar. This process is called photosynthesis.

Horse chestnut

Veins carry water to the leaves and sugar away from them.

Every leaf on the tree is a working food factory!

Leaf shapes

Take a look at all these leaves. Are they simple, compound, or needles?

sweet chestnut

silver birch

red maple

common beech

common holly

Douglas Fir

silk tree

rowan

weeping willow

buckeye

THE TREE HUNT CHALLENGE

Collect leaves

Make leaf rubbings or press the leaves to make cards.

Flowers

All trees produce flowers – though some are so small you would hardly notice them! Flowers have male and female parts. The male parts, called stamens, make pollen. The female parts, called ovaries, contain ovules. An ovule can grow into a seed if it is reached by pollen from another flower. This is called pollination. The pollen is blown by the wind or carried by insects.

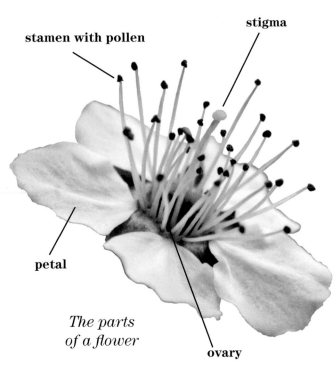

stamen with pollen

stigma

petal

ovary

The parts of a flower

Cherry tree

Bees visit flowers for their nectar. Pollen rubs onto their bodies, then rubs off on flowers from other trees.

Male and female

Some trees have flowers with both male and female parts. They are called perfect flowers. Other trees have separate male and female flowers. Can you identify the six perfect flowers (a–f)? To help you, we've shown them in full below. Which three flowers below aren't perfect?

Perfect flowers close-up

a b c

d e f

almond · apricot · tulip tree · willow

holly · laburnum · plum · walnut · cherry

Conifer flowers

Most conifers have separate male and female flowers on the same tree. The wind carries the dusty pollen to the female flowers, so their ovules can grow into seeds. Each female flower turns into a hard, woody cone. When the seeds are ripe, the cone opens and the seeds flutter away.

Fruits and seeds

Trees grow many kinds of fruit. The fruit develops from the female flower and contains the seeds. Some fruits have just one seed and some have lots. Fruits protect seeds while they grow. Sometimes, they also help seeds to spread once they are ripe.

Fruits from broad-leaved trees include nuts, berries, apples, and pears. These are a tasty treat for birds and other animals. They eat the fruit and poo out the seeds later.

This helps the seeds find a place to grow away from the parent tree. Conifer fruits are usually scaly cones, but junipers and yews produce berry-like fruits instead.

Inside the yew tree's fleshy red cups are a small green seed.

Horse chestnut tree fruits are called conkers. A prickly case protects them while they develop.

All kinds of fruit

Can you match each fruit to the right tree?

crab apple

horse chestnut

figs

dates

pear

rowan berries

a

b

c

d

e

f

THE TREE HUNT CHALLENGE

Do a blind fruit tasting test

• • • • • • • • • • • • • • • • •

How many fruits can you identify?

Measuring trees

When you are a nature hunter, it is useful to know details such as the height of trees. Ask a friend to stand by the tree. Stand a distance away, holding a pencil so its top and its bottom line up with your friend's head and feet. Standing in the same spot, see how many pencils match the height of the tree. Times this number by your friend's height to work out how tall the tree is.

Knowing the distance around the trunk helps you guess the tree's age. Every 1 inch (2.5 cm) equals a year's growth.

Tall and small

Take a look at these trees. Match them to the outlines below. Can you put them in order of size?

crab apple

giant sequoia

English oak

common ash

a
100-131 feet
(30-40 m)

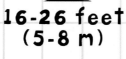
b
16-26 feet
(5-8 m)

c
65-115 feet
(20-35 m)

d
164-279 feet
(50-85 m)

Rings of growth

Counting the rings of a cut tree trunk tells you how old the tree was. Each ring represents one layer of sapwood and the tree grows a new layer of sapwood (see page 15) every year.

A cross-section of a tree trunk, showing its rings

Forests

Forests are amazing habitats. Trees provide protection from bad weather, wind, or too much sun. Their fallen leaves make the soil rich. Their roots hold the soil in place. All this encourages plants to grow. Fungi grow on rotting trunks and branches. Trees also provide food and shelter for many animals. There are bats and birds, deer, foxes, and rabbits. Countless creatures live in the forest, too.

Pine martens live in pine forests.

Broad-leaved forests often have a carpet of flowers in spring, before the trees' leaves block out the light. Forests of conifers have fewer plants on the ground because of the thick layer of needles and the lack of light.

Woodland phlox flowers in North American forests in early summer

Animal homes

Trees provide shelter for many woodland animals. Can you match the home to the animal?

 pine marten

bat

 little owl

squirrel

badger

a

b

c

d

e

THE TREE HUNT CHALLENGE

Walk in a forest

What animals can you see? Look for clues such as footprints or droppings.

Pests and fungi

Many insects use trees for food and shelter. They also lay their eggs in or around trees, so their young will have food to eat when they hatch. Sometimes, they damage the trees. They munch through leaves, wood, and roots or suck the sap. Plants can weaken the tree, too. Mistletoe and ivy grow on trees and can stop the leaves being able to make food.

This tree has been smothered by ivy. Eventually, the ivy will kill the tree.

Insect pests

Unjumble the names of these insect pests.

nipe evilwe

lem karb leteeb

nett laterparlic

feal remin

clue box
If you get stuck, you can find the unscrambled names here.

nut weevil
gall wasp
tent caterpillar
cherry fruit fly
elm bark beetle
black turpentine beetle
leaf miner
pine weevil

tnu wevlie

lagl paws

Fungi

Fungi are plant-like living things, such as mushrooms. Unlike plants, they cannot make their own food. They feed off other living things instead. Some fungi can kill trees. Dutch elm disease is caused by a fungus. It is spread by elm bark beetles.

This is bracket fungus. Under the bark, it makes the tree's heartwood rot.

The end of a tree

Trees have extraordinary life spans! They can live for hundreds or even thousands of years. During that time, there is wear and tear. Sometimes the bark is harmed when animals gnaw or scrape at it. Strong winds or lightning may break off branches or even split the trunk.

A fallen-down tree may carry on growing. This one's branches have become new "trunks."

Sometimes the tree can heal itself. If a branch breaks, the tree grows a special layer of bark to seal off the cut. This keeps out fungus and disease. Trees die if fungus or disease get in and spread. They also die if they run out of light or nutrients. But even a dead, rotting tree is still an amazing habitat.

This bristlecone pine is around 5,000 years old! It's called Methuselah.

Rotten critters

millipede

beetle

spider

earthworm

woodlouse

In broad-leaved trees, the leaves "die" every year. The carpet of rotting leaves beneath the trees, called leaf litter, is home to many creatures.

Can you match each close-up below to the whole creature?

a

c

b

e

d

THE ★ TREE HUNT ★ CHALLENGE

Hunt bugs in a rotten tree trunk

. . . .

How many kinds can you find?

Puzzle answers

5 Tree groups

coconut – palm
oak – broad-leaved
European larch – conifer
beech – broad-leaved
date palm – palm
Norway spruce – conifer
Scots pine – conifer
Japanese maple – broad-leaved
lime – broad-leaved

7 Seasons and trees

cherry – spring
horse chestnut – spring
American beech – autumn
lime – summer
hornbeam – winter
black poplar – autumn

9 Conifers up close

a – 1; b – 3; c – 2

11 Typical shapes

Norway spruce – d
cedar of Lebanon – e
Lombardy poplar – b
English oak – c
weeping willow – a
conifers: cedar of
Lebanon and Norway
spruce

13 Brilliant bark

a – zelkova elm
b – paper-bark maple
c – silver birch
d – European beech
e – rainbow eucalyptus

15 Winter buds

elm – e
alder – a
magnolia – f
beech – d
wild cherry – g
walnut – b
sycamore – c

17 Leaf shapes

sweet chestnut – simple
silver birch – simple
red maple – simple
common beech – simple
common holly – simple
silk tree – compound
rowan – compound
Douglas fir – needles
weeping willow – simple
buckeye – compound

19 Male and female

a – almond
b – apricot
c – cherry
d – tulip tree
e – plum
f – laburnum
The holly, walnut, and willow
are not perfect flowers.

21 All kinds of fruit

crab apple – e
horse chestnut – c
fig – d
date – b
pear – f
rowan berry – a

23 Tall and small

crab apple – b
giant sequoia – d
English oak – a
common ash – c
Size order: b c a d

25 Animal homes

pine marten – a
badger – b
bat – c
squirrel – d
little owl – e

27 Insect pests

a – pine weevil
b – elm bark beetle
c – tent caterpillar
d – nut weevil
e – leaf miner
f – gall wasp

29 Rotten critters

millipede – b
beetle – e
earthworm – c
spider – d
woodlouse – a

Glossary

bark The outside of a tree's trunk.

broad-leaved Describes a tree that has flat leaves and seeds contained in fruits, such as nuts and berries.

chlorophyll A green-colored chemical in leaves that takes in energy from sunlight.

compound leaf A leaf made up of smaller parts, called leaflets.

conifer A kind of tree that has needle-like or scaly leaves and seeds in fruits called cones.

coppice To cut a tree's trunk down to the ground to encourage new growth.

deciduous Describes a tree that sheds its leaves, usually in autumn.

dormant In a kind of sleep.

evergreen Describes a tree that keeps its leaves all year round.

fruit A ripened ovary that contains seeds. The fruit protects the seeds and may help them to spread.

fungus A plant-like living thing that cannot make its own food. Mushrooms and toadstools are fungi.

germinate To start to grow when conditions are right.

habitat A place where animals and plants live in the wild.

heartwood The old, dead wood at the center of a tree trunk.

leaflet A small separate part of a leaf.

lifespan The length of time that a living thing lives.

native Growing in or originating from a particular place.

ovary The female part of a flower that contains developing seeds.

ovule A female cell in a plant, which can develop into a seed if it is pollinated.

perfect flower A flower that has stamens (male) and an ovary (female).

photosynthesis The way trees and other plants make food energy when their chlorophyll reacts with sunlight, carbon dioxide, and water to make sugars.

pollard To cut off a tree's branches to encourage new growth.

pollen Dust-like particles that contain a plant's male cells.

pollination When pollen reaches an ovule and it can start to grow into a seed.

prune To cut.

sap The fluid that carries water, nutrients, and sugars around a tree or other plant.

sapwood The new, living wood at the outer edge of a tree trunk, just under the bark.

simple leaf A leaf that is not divided into separate parts.

stamen The male part of a flower that holds the pollen.

Index

websites

PowerKids Press has developed an online list of websites related to the subject of this book. This site is updated regularly. Please use this link to access the list:
www.powerkidslinks.com/ain/trees